Added here from last pages of Notebook

We learn to understand others before we understand the self.

in relation
mapping

Anaximenes saw the soul as embodying self-propelled motion.
For Pythagoras form is identical with soul, matter with body.
He ennobled the soul with divine origins.

Does the soul contain the body then? shape it? act as vehicle?

Plato: (Meno)—The Soul has lived before.
    (Phaedras)—The Soul has no beginning and can never
    have an end.

When the soul entered the body it filled the vase like water.

The word soul is feminine in Greek, Latin, Arabic, German
and all the romance languages.

           — ?

2nd Century A.D. a beautiful female Orante on the crypt ceiling
at Lucina.

His house is destroyed by fire and he becomes occupied in
rebuilding it.

"Here we have no abiding City"—Hildebert of Lavardin

We have a single, emaciated man lying on an embroidered cloth
in an open landscape.

A corollary of guilt is punishment.

According to More the soul has an *Airy Body*.

Still the reader asks "But what type of body?"

Returning to the meadow the *Soul* a shaft of light.

City

It is the iteration between body and brain that is consciousness.

In the portrait of the imagined viewer no wind moves the cloak.

Mysteries and corn stand side by side.

iteration:
the repetition of a process or utterance.
rehearsal?...
⌐→ goal

Should this
be taken at face
value?

prose—discus

English Fragments *A Brief History of the Soul*

English Fragments *A Brief History of the Soul*

MARTIN CORLESS-SMITH

ALBANY, NEW YORK

Book design by Rebecca Wolff

Published in the United States by Fence Books, Science Library, 320
University at Albany, 1400 Washington Avenue, Albany, NY 12222,
www.fenceportal.org

Fence Books are printed in Canada by Westcan Printing Group and
distributed by Consortium Book Sales and Distribution.

Library of Congress Cataloguing in Publication Data
Corless-Smith, Martin [1965-]
English Fragments A Brief History of the Soul / Martin Corless-Smith

Library of Congress Control Number: 2010937693

ISBN 13: 978-1-934200-38-4

FIRST EDITION
10 9 8 7 6 5 4 3 2

Fence Books are published in partnership with the University at
Albany and the New York State Writers Institute, and with help from
the New York State Council on the Arts and the National Endowment
for the Arts.

The Author wishes to thank those publications where some of these
poems have previously appeared in print. "Onsets," *A Breviary of Poems
13 lines or under* (The Gig); "From: The Dialogue of the Sunne and the
Moone," A Gargoyle Edition, Sheffield, England 2004; "A dark disc is
gulped down," Skanky Possum Broadside, Austin, Texas, November
2004; "Hic Jacet," A Gargoyle edition, Sheffield, England, October
2003; "Diurnal" Broadside, Evergreen State College, May 2005. And
journals: *Barrowstreet, Colorado Review, Electronic Poetry Review, Fence,
New American Writing, Parcel* and *Phoebe.*

For Romayne Licudi

Hic Jacet

Thus at their shady lodge arrived
Only of grass clung to a mould of clay
But as it hurled to this one place
The world managed in its finite parts
To mime infinity—a glass contrived
Artfully placed to show the world its face.

—T. S.

mirror
reflection
mimicking?
deceit?
duplication...

Thomas Swan?

The soul conceived in God's alembic flesh
—Th^{os.} Swan

legend needed.

math? temperature reading?

Thomas Swan?

Dark Matter

For (matter) he has made my soul
Just as a mirror (is) held up to a room
For how (else) (to) else know thyself/hisself
And in so doing a dark otherness

Soul is the ever-expanding surface of experience
—William Williamson

why here?

open ↓
(I am become a monster to myself) tense
Sad age creep up on me
to sag and ravage mind diction
Where do we take it now

I am a monster to myself
when now this body is this shape
how does another face take this
I look across to you to speak
and am contrariness itself beautiful

a head puffed up by parasites
your young limbs passed unopened
we have haven't we
all been going for a while

fortune or virtue or wisdom both,
are little else than shiftless beasts
before the rash and inconsiderate
A head requiring hellebore musical
to call this honest house

Where else for you or me
I have let go
I have forgotten what I let go of
I look across to you to speak
Close And have become a monster to myself

hellebore: a poisonous winter-flowering plant.

5

Aristotle conceived *Soul* to be the activity of the body. In the case of objects that involve no matter, what thinks and what is thought are identical.

What was/is the activity of the soul?

local in his throne the nameless He (World)
suspended here indefinite, indefinitely
spans an immense universe—the night sky
and the night we do not see
the book a prostrate ANGEL and extended DEITY
the lashes of closed eyes engraven
midway in eternity
our waking dreams are fatal—born
on a collapsing wave perpetually

—W. W.

I was terrified at finding myself in the middle of nothing, myself a nothing. I felt as though I was suffocating as I pondered and experienced the fact that all is nothing, solid nothing ✳
—Leopardi, *Zibaldone*

Either there is the experience of the present action without self-consciousness (in which case me is not presented to the conscious faculty) or the object of contemplation is a remembered or a predicted presence. "Time paradox".

At the centre of being is a nothingness that only the next act avoids (infinite finitudes).

✳ "Nothing outside can cure you but everything's outside".

→ nothing inside. nothing can cure you, but the things that heal or don't. Its about space. Its not a statement about

I repeat: All is dead, whole worlds
And lost the falling Milky Way
so far as life, in its veins
spills dark sand on abandoned waves

Everywhere the desert sun the page
confuses oceans scrawled
in wandering
nothing exists anywhere

The searching eye of God—a socket
blind—black—without night
rays on the world all day

A rainbow turns down
past old chaos, shadow
Spirals out the world in play

(after de Nerval, *Les Chimères*).

Space is the soul's to inhabit
—Swinburne, *Hymn of Man*

Feeling the threshold of being to be both the experience (poem) and the coming-into-history of that experience (prose).

time paradox

Self-sameness and otherness simultaneously.

Each word sets forth (leaving a trace).

The janus-faced doorway.

- The poem is an allegory of being that turned out to be. The object will make shadows unwittingly.

- Its being written and its being read.

The poet (exiled from the city) exiles himself from the city. Sends his missive to another city (abandons it in passing).

difference?

In our expanding universe the poem never manages to catch up with the reader—or to reach the author.

vs. reader w/ poem

the reader? or the poem?

(The past and the future are beyond us, and the present self does not exist at all).

Narrative is the history of consolation.

I've written this before
I meant to.
However quickly it happens.

meta

what about: consolation is the history of narrative.

12

City

In Romayne's Garden, June 5th 2003

When in the evening beetles
Hang the green sky in between
Great plum great cherry trees
Grown slowly upwards yards in to the green
Mantle screen—our misty gauze is momentarily
lifted as a cherry amber buzzing
ar electric animal.

The comedy opens
simple violence—incontinence—malice
Add these to unbelief or misbelief
Add again the circle outside the River Acheron (the Thames)

The Year of the Vision is 1300
The sun is rising on Friday morning
The moon sets (noon Jerusalem time)

Again in the middle of everything
Ah!
(defecating in a cell of defecation)

The birds hard at it—Under the cherry boughs
in my shade—(anybody else's true)
for all I care
How long have I been this silent (have I been)

Tick of the wren—the warbling Robin underfoot
Words I repeat. Words I have heard another sing more gracefully.
Why do you carry on their burdens/songs/their deeds
A Robin at his seed

The great city outside the Walls
roars on a pace—and I have come to fall in quietude
my home between heres
seated hopefully—but we have given everything (away)

The Robin feeds
made in our own image (How can we imagine otherwise?)

The labour and strife of the soul is as vivid and earnest as any bodily travail

old
text?...

Soul + body

A Light messenger
Light may replace us—assail us/Light may replace the self —*musical*
Lifting the dark(ness) that we cannot
none of the Earth was ever so blessed

The light is not ours. Our selfhood we experience it—but it is not ours.

a flash of silver (   )
(The) blackbirds (noisy) noise
Can you hear his misery?
I feel a coward's fear.

Upon the river which is of the sea
Through me into the city
(Along the river path,
the wretched and the wealthy pass)

The World has glory over them
An ancient shouting by the banks
the other side is autumn
with its spoils upon the ground

a light drizzle in the foliage
visible as terror yields
to sadness for my child and for myself
holding him

blind swallows skirt the house
a thousand colours nearly visible
and you might call to them
as they whirr in company

a black air—or a magnificent green
The red-eyed fly upon behemoth beans
if we knew who to ask

The town where I was born
Sits with its river and canal
underneath is everything
a body falls continually

a book who kissed my mouth
the spirit speaking through the body
a canal
and heavy rain

descending far enough to see

The fearful passage and the continuance

If I can see the Ocean anywhere it's here
Step out off the skiff into the plunging buoyancy
(I had thought to carry on along the surface to some finer spot)
(my Self remained without)

He had his eyes upon the ground
City of Dis or Pluto
Like with like is buried here
Famous (for its town and) amphitheatre
                    ?

Violence may be done against the deity
In the heart denying him
disdaining nature—consumed in the fat marsh
Beasts the rain beats

—W. W.

The soul for example—may it not, withstanding, lie in the porch, at the gate of the Temple called beautiful, and be a door-keeper in the house of its God?

((This is not my house))

he in the middle
who is looking down upon his breast
locking and unlocking so the (soft and) broken splint

the spirit quits the body
briefly whenever
a grain of spelt
a sapling-tree

he therefore resumed
then the wind turned into words
which thus disjoined my leaves from me

Officers (off he soars?) cavort
All heaven (all having?) a torn garment
Hysterical (his terror calls?) running and falls (anvils?)
A honey bird pinned in the wheat

feels like he's
telling us too much

Dean Prior—Devon (Downpour)

Carswash onto Plymouth
Where we stop (into) a dark and quiet church
Dedicatory air the young girls
All around here smile

A wooden closet fastend shut
Behind the pulpit by the aisle
(If I had rhymes I heard no voice)
(All my hidden ocean boils)

Eventually after a long eulogizing sentence
The poet's name
Among sane men
who had disproved most things
And proved the rest
He was possessed of
a fervour and a fury of belief
Without a clue for the hand
Or a feature for the eye
What he meant, what he wanted

Tea-pot pieties and tape-yard infidelities
It is not his art we envy but his belief
It is not his vision we desire but his certainty
The remnants of an invaluable quality of actual life

A hasty disguise rigged to no end

It is a time of plague
And great injustice
I singe my beard
And panic out my hairs

I wear the shirt I had been given
As it fits
The whole enfolded city
Fires all over Europe

Naturally enough the satiated species consumes itself.

Loving makes change unbearable. When the old building passes into disuse and is eventually pulled down—to make way for new houses—we are burdened with (the responsibility of) its memory. We must know that our memories have become their own world—not holding closely to this one.

In this section of underwall which remains damp even in high summer under the elm canopy with always the deep rich odour of cake moist earth.

What does it matter that someone considers himself worthy? I shall be what energy allows. What my dreams of these avenues—of the deep pond—means, as themselves—part of my vision lifts and rests upon the just ingredients.

All morning with sketch book in hand—leave the rivers to themselves. Return to the avenues.

The erotic expectation. A brooding figure. It is the self watching over me. I brush past this figure trailing a hand but the self cannot be charmed or seduced. There in the mirror, behind the voyeur is a steely gaze. We know.

My creation/frustration why my chest heaves in anguish is to be done with all this ordering and solving. The monotonous shifting of objects on the shelf. Even this one view, this ordinary Victorian terrace window, out to an overgrown garden, even this is beyond my every effort magnified a hundred life times. The agapanthus is otherworldly, the quince is faintly ridiculous, the buddleia a gaudy mess, and I am a stew of vanity and foolishness—my miracle is all that which I cannot affect. My greatest part is that of which I can take no credit.

I am tender about the friends I dreamt of last night—remembering our night time collaboration my heart moves as I walk along I am in love the street goes on marching through my vision down to the Thames where we all drown in unison. That is it about the Thames it overwhelms our stories. Even the tales of the drowned are kept secret, the bridge continues underwater but it is the reflection we see.

Later I will meet my wife and child in town. How can this be? How can this have happened?

something very raw

(Bury the house opposite)

When a mediocre building is knocked down, we are gripped by a
fear.

Found in the basement. Many are cleverer than me—so I can only
do this, be myself, that's the best thing I can do—try to relax a little
found in the basement hunched a few days later, having not left
the flat it became more difficult to face the possibilities—falling off
one's pavement walk into the territory of others—their own terror
transformed to hatred meted out in a stride you are supposed to
repel. Nettles and newspapers. No one in the allotments hears
over the broadcast of cricket and the railway tracks hunched into
a praying squat—ready to implode. Poppies and swan manage
deportment amongst the trash. Poppies on the wasteland—swans
in the canal. Morphine seduction. Greek passion. Milk and teabags.
There is no place for God without a daily branding of fear.

The ambassadors are liars—our servants overseas
How can we believe ourselves
far from the human, far from home
the ocean underneath a ship

How do you even manage
As part of the Republic
Mugged, mobb'd and robb'd
Out-institutioned

Ex-Arcady routine
The great western robbery
Your calm belingered by
The green trench woods

Tumultuous versions
Quite put out
Really popular version
Of this quit spirit
You'd not even recognize
The face of God or Love
If she peeked through the hedge
Offering herself
Anima climax
Mismanaged outfit
No legs in these trousers
Get home stay there

Let us hope for more sunshine and an increase only marginal in our wealth over others. Building continues unabated. My energy sexes through the hallways past dressing strangers up into attic sublets. Parsimonious and grim. Mustachioed recluses and their tuna rolls. Egg and Cress. Every moment someone agrees with something out of weakness or despair. Even a harried rap at the door doesn't really matter. Urgency is acquired.

I might be out of all visible things.

Awaken to the trickle and sob of the sleeping cat

Charmed into exile
Some instinct of return

Bells supra urbem, the dismembered ecstasy above the whole city. We who have invited into our nests the end of our lives. The loathed pigeons crowding, the occasional mad peacock, the occasional embracing couple, thinly veiled youth, the (occasional) smile. Or child. Disturb us. momentarily and pass.

1918

Just two adults consenting at pleasure. How difficult can that be? What you might describe as ideal. Or rare even.

All our secrets are insignificant. The triumphant pederast in the corner. Our species is tattooed over our swollen flesh. It is not shyness, it is not dignity, it is fatigue and ignorance. The best friend enters the dream. She has decided to allow him to seduce her. From behind you are to feel for her wet and her warm. At present we must hope she does not demur—recasting your advances as an intrusion. In the dream this opening pass is played out again and again *ad infinitum*. The door opens to her swagger. Can't a bit of fun be had? And again the door opens and she enters the room.

The city falling does not stop at my skin. The weather and the people are within me—my slow motion mania can do nothing, my crouch end and my bow bells my highgate and my hammersmith. my life. my creature.

beyond the boundaries of skin

Routine renders us amnesiac
A change of dressing
Nights in the chamber
Sir Francis Drake drunk in a coracle.

Stirring behind the curtain is a field of corn.

Midges over the pool—they are feeble and marvelous and gone in the instant. The rare bird I followed into the woods to see is a common woodcock.

Reflection on the windowpane. Air in the curtains. Avenue of rooming houses. What did I have? A bag of clothes, some handful of books, most of the paintings to follow at a later date, because as of this morning I am uncertain where I'll be staying. Heaven and hell revolve on a thread. Skies filled with unspeakable colours. If I have drunk too much, if I have wasted the morning in agonies.

The old gods were dying. Demeter with her lovely hair ignored, and the shears loosely held, hacked and snipped her to a disfigured corpse. Mars was powerful but no longer eloquent. Chaos alone was profiting. But Chaos could not sustain us. I have no work. I have fashioned a profession out of the accidents of my education. My relationships have mostly foundered from no rightful approach and an overwhelming desire to have them done and finished.

Flowers of the field
The Poppy tribe
Soon falling off
Under the name of Opium
Laudanum and Morphia
But its native country is unknown

It is the case that we might forget our former selves, but they accompany us.

I occupied a life I was not leading. A vast Victorian kitchen where I have ascended to the ceiling, and am now my own ghost—pitifully spread out above and below, waiting.

The powers of the soul may be said to be a medium between substance and accident.

Each spill manages itself to the ocean. The snatches of garden and parkland in the city might likewise be hopeful of a unified primeval forest. None of us should have done any better.

My meat is picked open—the eyes are meery. I'm lurching into perversions through boredom. My considerableness is past mustering. The life-threatening treat—A death agony. I have made some moves to be here. Habeas corpus. Everything we experience is exact, but it does not mean, nor can it mean anything else exactly…the sky is very precise, a description of which might itself be very precise, but the sky and the description are altogether different occurrences. This will not stop us hoping for some vital link.

between layers
between language and life

October 11ᵗʰ, 2003 the white houses are buzzing in blues and lavender. And orange berries fill the height of the front garden. All of this, a son in bliss. I can't.

Three ages of history (as described by Marcus Terentius Varro, the greatest scholar of Roman antiquities, in his great work, now lost, entitled Divine and Human Institutions)

1) *the mythical age (childhood, nostalgia)*
2) *the dark age, in which all have dispensed of knowing (transition of Epochs/Empires—fear entrenched in ignorance)*
3) *the historical age.*

During my Second and Third childhood in the Chiswick Garden, near to the Thames (Corot), a motion of rotation and stillness. Allotments (Constable) by the playing fields. Somewhere a fire, an alarm, a quick quiet apologetic fucking, roll on roll off without congress or intimate release. The transubstantiation of celebrity into deity—a pixilated face broadcast in satellite. Sacrifice. Our night thoughts have the bodies to themselves.

All undergone in the secret cradle of our weakness and strength.

None of my lives are over. I can barely attend the portion most evident. Even a greater capacity for work and a greater faculty of memory would allow me only clues to the complex of selves bustling in existence (as many minds would find as many selves). Consciousness produces itself in the instant with its eyes on the now while our selves swim at the periphery. We reach after them, placing names and dates as memorials.

The voice of the cup on the table yelling, the plates ringing and troughing. All of the furniture composing its perfect tune—a chorus of sorts—columns of space arched around windows and door—the ocean buoyed on light and air.

Aging is a diminution of our willingness to live. Fear and containment replace the wandering excesses. We die by the facts of our existence. The terrible thing about being a writer is that it is what I wanted. There is nothing else to hope for.

Sonnet written at Wentworth Place, November 5th, 2003

I went to write a sonnet in this house
How his young blood left stains
Please mind your head
And breath upon the window pane
A speculative builder (built) on a 99-year lease
Based on the need to carry out repairs
When Keats was built in 1814–15 winter of
Looking grander by design
Please do not sit here!
The chimney stacks, the guttering, the roof
Rendered, slate, Plaque, Door
Coffer Roof—strengthening the upper floor
How do we know what colour paint to use
Upstairs—re-laid in its position on a lime mortar.

Marriage, burial and the division of fields
An urn placed to one side in the forest (assuming location)
D. M. (Dis Manibus—the good souls of the buried dead)
Pursuing shy intractable women

A plough emerges from the forest where the urn is placed
Its handle rests against an altar with a certain prominence
The cities cultivated where the trees were felled
Rome opened in a clearing

Finally the rudder is at some distance from the plough

A strong part of me endures for that life I do not lead

And I'm trying not to lie, even in the pompous way I say this.

Some are said to carry the palaces of gods on their backs, while others are believed to determine the course of streams and rivers and feed on pearls.

repeat pg. 44

Not to be known. (Faces) reflections in the windowpane—Air in
the curtains—an avenue of rooming houses. What did I have? A
bag of clothes—some handful of books—volumes of poetry—
most of the paintings to follow at a later date. Because as of this
morning I am uncertain where I will be staying. Heaven and hell
revolve on a thread.

In front of the river scene we are nonexistent unless we dissolve into articulation. The sorrowful dwellings (really?) that are shells merely—the tethered boats—the river police's brightly painted shed upon the floating jetty—these nod and tremble innocent of need, made into characters peopling an inaudible dialogue.

from: The Dialogue of the *Sunne* and the *Moone*

The words being to be understood
according to the minds engraved
as if God knifed the very wood
of us {as God in Christ is saved
upon the wood} our name
is shown in shining Gold
our Soul which is the same
as God's own voice as told
in dialogue subordinate to it
where he describes without
the Sun as to the Moon is
in a sky behind the cloud...

(Quoted in this part from the manuscript of Nathaneal
Culverwell's *Discourse of the Light of Nature*)

...like so many natural automata
believing them the principles of their own motion
laid this down as if (var. to be) a written axiom
But where is it (var. he) that carved the moon
{Who cannot even read the mood
of one such maid of (var. as) Great Diana}
Souls they move themselves
and they move bodies actually
Reason, Religion, Laws and Prudence
wind ruling (in) the Forest leaves
the (var. in) contrivance of the eternal word

spoken through the wisdome of our Lord
conditions and dimensions once
defined like many instruments allow
the variant anthematic to translate
from a whisper to bellow (from) his own breath...

—T. S.

The man with his throat cut
Has awoken to his dead self
His misfortune. Being already lost
If I would only remember

Hold onto that—but as in sleep
The dream was its own purpose
Not mine for recollection
Or living/life to be evoked by care

*our dreams
are not for
our sake ...*

It is odd that he recalls
Some incidental people
A woman who was not his lover
And a child in a distant city or town

And these clothes
When did he dress?
This morning only
But so long ago these shoes
Where did they come from

He forgets the light and sounds
He forgets the feel of the ground before him
The board beneath his back

My body casts a shadow (shade)
But what sunne/sonne has cast itself
And moulded here by means some how (and here made)
Of other worldly light between the spirit
And its show—An Ocean some swift bay
The Moon in countenance enhances night
By measuring the dark elsewhere
And is the solid gift of flesh
Acts as a beacon for his eye(s)
Spilt in a universe of light

—T. S.

How shall a modest love be had
The dark house stands in a darker field
The cuckoo plaints its seasonal
And nothing will oppose the fates

from The History of the Human Race

We are told they were nourished by bees
in infancy—community held—coincidental.
The passing of cars and a people
Incidentally after little sleep
And alcohol—the clarity of recent loss
Dull residue of unresolved anxieties
Friends—which can mean pleasant strangers

In idea of the Son predicts the Moone
The Ocean sounds but nowhere on the land
And quiet in its depths the Whale moans
And vessels on the surface feel her sound

—T. S.

At the uncanny river's edge
I dreamt a dream of life and death
One wave subsuming and subsumed
Upon the slowly shifting bank

—T. S.

dreams

this kind of movement parallels

The cupboard opens with a gasp
I must in part be housed in there
I know too frequently the rub of wood
On wood

—W. W.

If I have anything to say I must surely be saying it.

Can you find anything but here?

)aware

From the French Argot

When the invaders pillaged our abandoned tombs
We had plundered ourselves exactly
As they. Made in the defiling effigy
the various frosted gods—like stains upon the bed

*

The partial truth of the above stanza
Is not dishonest. It manages for a while
To distract us both from the inevitable

A short moment in the Arbutus
The Strabo—The Graffo or Crespa
The Bardo—I don't know anywhere

Darlings! Who is it I enjore?

*

we shut up doors against the flood
which is no good
all over town the waxwings finish berries off the trees
we pour outside to witness spring
in peels of lethargy and glee

Now that window
for example
It could be happiness
or sorrow

a rose came by my line
a name I call her by
across to that which I
can never see again

so softly light the ear
ring nightly round our day
which hour we recall
yet hover when we hear

iambic tetrameter?.

that is on the trembling tree
still reminds me of one morning
the night in rain til the next day
yet let me God live long enough
that I may have my hands of her
or a brief word that spreads itself
As in a season fresh and new
We don't see the messenger ─────────
Nor whether he is questioned for
Thus with a letter
Our love goes thus

Sonnet?

Under a hedge the other day
When I arrived by accident
And will not joy come follow me
A shepherd full of merriment

I close my eyes against the world
Against my own heartbrokenness
But rain is sure to dampen me
And where she lives I cannot see

Should I recover of myself
Sometime emerge into the light
It will not be because of sun
But as my bones are washed so white

My Angel has abandoned me
And I must take her part in this

The cabin rags our favourite clothes
Green clothes us and the elemental storm
Rain in our kettle rain in our socks
For centuries now over the stream

Life is a pure flame, and we live by an invisible sun within us
—Sir Th^os. Browne.

Conceive light invisible and that is spirit
—Sir Th^os. Browne.

The soul dwells within us, a flame the size of a thumb
—Katha Upanishad.

Ardent vehicle—ornately called
In Flame! The sparse rose field
Never lives in speech chimes
Or place one hand by the bell

To scald your name my rhyme
Lung fall, the Tyne, the Nile
The scalped Atlantic carries

(a door?) in touch and four
worlds pacific
the mountains part the sea circles mounts
the Pennines part the sea circles the Alps

(Petrarch 146)

translating?"

When violets search on dew
Enduring friend my mean rag memory
Transparent time or useless leg
Perfect in part my spirit is content

(find the poor glittering
deep hollow near the front
a green love—impressive courage
further nor torment my ear

End of colour—culprit time
Irrational Jove retires
His grand desire afraid
Across light come and tailor raise your view)

(Petrarch 147)

(As speech is the index of the soul, the soul governs speech) The one depends upon the other: The former lies hidden in our breast, the latter goes outside; the soul prepares speech to go outwards and moulds it as it wants it to be, and speech, coming forth, manifests what the soul is.
—Petrarch, *To Tommaso da Messina*

Chambers draws attention to the "circumambient penumbra of spirituality in which Laura is veiled."

Reflections of a poor eye

The viaduct, the Aqueduct called Telford's Aqueduct at Chide
The stream supports a shadow where reflections lie
Spread near the foliage of indigenous varieties
Where are the walkers, where our fellow sufferers?

The sun, which we can know of in extent
Seeks out in its enormity one side
Its ulterior effect is this colossal
Where we reap a noon and sow a shade

But I am prone to shadows, anxious matter in its dance
Consoles and Lunges after emptiness, and properties defile
   the fields
excellent midnight, the shade of surplus agency, which drains
Heaven, makes a promise of the virtual or real.

The sheep-child in buoyant carriage
On the waves? The image is so bronzed
With pastoral memory, the child, the blankets
And the mist of water over her.

Elegy for the worm

so drastic

Vermiculate who ate
itself—(no) beginning
middle end—and saddled
with the passing earth
rained out devoured
Our soul's content

Soul
earth
elements

The soul...has become only an unbroken endless hearkening: spread out to infinity, infinitely held in the orbit of time, infinite in her repose...along with the landscape which is herself...on the surface of which the spheres of heavenly light and earthly darkness part one from the other, she is like them in being the border, separating and binding the regions above and below, belonging like Janus to both, to those of the wavering stars as well as to those of the weighty stones, to the etheric regions as well as the fires of the underworld, januslike the double aspect of infinity, januslike the double aspect of the soul...

—Hermann Broch, *The Death of Virgil*

dualities
multiplicities

fires erupt continuously WOE & WOE
and I cannot then batter down
FLUSH and FLAME sat where I am
at the table arms inert upon a spectre
FLASH and WOE all about my case

a list of contagencies burn & burn burn
& WOE again arizing a medieval home
which Fire has been used to purify & vivify
and to ordain or divinate—and I do not know Flames
or knowing water only in its element

I am invited to oxygen and to cold air between Elms
and warm currents hover over crops
and I am contiguous with green boughs & green branches
and the movement of the moist green leaf tacky unfurls

Rattle of brittle claws for months
In the town some mornings bells blow in
I go shopping for the ingredients
which is the news all this is the news

My home is over a trudging field
which weight I carry on my boots
And by the door this frozen threshold yields
leave them outside left them out of doors

drama
cues → noises
effects

77

Gun crack out of the woods
all through the air—crows up
trees resolute against the fear
Gun crack someone knows

—W. W., (*Ombersley*)

suspicious

mysterious

FLOWES FORWARD

Where here I come again
drip into house
bees against the window
slowly looking in

great forms moving in the darkness
the monoliths established in obscurity
(doing something rather for its own sake)
to be something out of all these parts

there are trees along the bank
that reach down underneath the river
and how far above us is their view
though their green eyes shudder

we cannot believe our lives
or even
this
our disrobing

constellations upon the river surface
upon the insect eyes
the foliage invariably stricken
wheels seen through the leaves

a stranger crucified
fish marvelous endure
twice in two days a dream
two nights in a row this aisle

instead of 'afterwards' instead of 'ask for him'
my sixty dollars buys
boiled woolen jacket
a bush erupts in finches

an unknown word FLASHES
mixing bowl reminding you
ownerless
I fail to understand

something so high that looked so small
has fallen to Earth and is Giant
mildew upon one acre of corn
A lot of people are talking

it is a kingdom; not only a house
if thine could carry thee so low
as to think that thou wert become some other this
a fish, a dog had fed upon

—W. W.

Entelechia

We fail to recognize ourselves outside
there is no point before this we should know
the mind revolving & divided by its sun
clouded in the instant of its skin

blood our selves leaks out
to show we have affected something are affected by
ourselves we cannot look we cannot help but look
cops buzz around excited by the show

a mountain falls today in purple
shadow and the basined town
like all other mortal things
words change and pass away

how bland attachment causes
every art made out of grief and hope
I would give up everything
Not to be with you

Another example would be the sun
try all you will to separate the light from it
forever the light is
in the sun

—W. W.

longing for distinction / yet

Mutability Chorus

Like to Narcissus on the grassy shore
seeing his outward face upon that face
as he looks still his face appears
under its surface an expressionless display

—fish beneath that one fish beneath this
expanse onto which we witness all
the surface beneath
or nothing above or—

I bent forward to see
the flame arrive
look
see, how toward it with desire I bend

I sailed into the illimitable main
with one cleav'd bark
as far as the next shore
where my companions where we came

refuse no proof of the unpeopled world
the mind of my associates our oars
our lows the ocean floor
Joy turned to morning the new land

suppose some reason had befallen
(there was reason to suppose)
explorers of the ocean
where we left ourselves

yes with eyes to follow them
I deserved you while I lived
I became the expert of the world
put me before the open sea

—W. W.

This office of fine bones
Curtain of flesh
Contains the articles of play
A manikin, a robe & props
Ignite with flautus—manifest
Engined by the light of day
Still, when we see them sit
Imagine that they house some wit
Indolent and silent in his little hut
A bird flits through the chamber
Lit with the sun's last amber rays
Then out, lost to the dark night of our eyes

—T. S.

Biblio mundi
Two weeks later
The dead now living
that we can never
Touch the soul's hem.

The 12 or 14 Stations

Melancholy   The grey cloth we crawl upon/featureless
terrain   Waterloo 8 AM

Surprise   The train door that bears our soul away/a
gust

Worry   what of ourself remains

Contentment   passing/thin bank at the river bend/wading
cattle

Anxiety   Roar of the approaching/news reaching the
valley   Night caller

Forgiveness   that we cannot of ourselves/or others

Regret   one moment decided/or another

Misery   Not to notice/that the rain we need is at our
heels

Sadness   leaves/returning home/ward journey

Happiness   jewel light on water/softly on the way

Anticipation   dressing/fruit trees for the festival

Hope   in Youth our energy

Misery	to turn away from the world
Regret	in age our energy ──
Hope	her message

Melancholia—the transference of the park, Dearest Antelope, the hart
is pierced—and trails the Royal Forest. Past beauty, youth, two student-
lovers drowned in the canal.

On waking/the form of living/indistinguishable from/meaning/
My brother opposite to this?/the underneath/relationship
Said for effect/because of me/because of this
The building where/lived/I used to live
My left-hand life/is entering the room/the other room
Our neighbour/natural antipathy/leaving for work
I remember to myself/to smile at pedestrians/like myself
London in August/London at Midnight/nobody's (London)
Boise in Journal/(Boise)discover/empty container
Janus in peril/Anguish of Infant/Mute Motorcyclist

25,000 Beautiful towns (he says)

How am I going to get away

My dreams of the future contain me.

The Day

If there is a self it hovers so close or so far from us that we cannot know it. That which we tell ourselves about ourselves might be useful about being, might be coincidental with some truth—but we cannot know. For truth also is so close or so far from us.

The Day (A 600 page poem written about one day)

The Dream opening
The acceptance of waking
Leaving the first room
Attending to food
Memories of earlier days
That which needs
The first half-capitulations
Dressing
Tasks
Sleep comes upon him
The tasks
The call
Awake and leaving
Interaction
Escape
The world
Confusion
Love
Intercourse
Retreat
The ambiguous
Loathing and loathed
Selfhood persistent
Fear of death (commitment)

Acknowledgement of Life
Sanctuaries
Work
Forgiveness / generosity
Happiness / tiredness / sadness
The formal retreat
Depletion of energies
The feast
Death

The Library Inferno

but are we supposed to ? ghosts so

[I do not believe in ghosts unless I see them.] I forget them.
I read, I need to find the necessary volume for the space. B⌐⌐⌐
quantity manifest our partial belief that nothing in the world passes
away. Nothing has disappeared. We apprehend very little. Ghosts
emerge in our peripheral vision. Today (meaningless) I could not
see anybody.

or neither

The library burned to the ground. Impossibly this always happens.
The grand and the modest cracked into ashes. The space we
inhabit has its permanence in our reflection. The collapsed library
is our monster of impermanence. Busts of the Emperors—those
whose focused approximations captivated for some time. When
the library dissolves in flames the river's indifference is a thrill.
The energy of the catastrophe doubles and trebles. The rubies
and lobster tails—peacock and jasmine flowers. The urge to speak
means that no silence and no statement is truly descriptive.

The book is one model of the possible (nonexistent) interior. When
we realize the self we have called into being is not touched by our
invocations the book is our only resort. It is neither ourself, nor our
consolation, nor strictly the articulation of our loss. If a book can
fail to articulate the truth then it must. The nightroom illuminated
in an infinitesimal (untraceable) tracing collage of sensations that
I turned into memory. Later, immediately, when I told myself the
story I knew even in its complicated structure, centuries of detail
had been incorrectly recorded. These details were the blood and
fibre of the lost. This landscape does not adhere.

My community is born of a self-preservation with no real intention
of my own glory. Survival comes before selfhood. Mediated reality
is real.

(The library cracks and wheezes like bright rain.)Augustus on the pilaster—Caesar on the balustrade, book hinges glow like breath—Menander shreds—Montaigne abolie. Towers of glass, shanks of wall the crystalline evaporation of a word—juice of a thousand armchairs—the Saxons and the Picts, Berserkers Vandals Ostragoths, the ruddy bearded Viking and the wire clad Celt. Where the store is was.

The Double Garden

Equal to our Domestic Garden—the herbarium enclosed by the
loggias—is that other Garden—existing precisely where our garden
is. Both Gardens seem inseparable. In one the hyacinth and jonquils
frisk etc., as in the other world amasses a description. On both
sides the garden bends out of view only to regroup behind us—as
if spinning made the world dimensional. When I began speaking
to the garden my choice of words is no longer unsettling—for the
words fly off and disperse so exactly that the gardens, so quietly
acquiescing, don't notice. Pay no attention to me. The garden
bending behind both of us.

The Evening of a Faun

Memories of an unread book.

Come join me more quietly. My days of chasing are past.

For the evening we will accept what we find—in the way of music and repast.

Some unearthed truffles, mountain garlic and a fowl or two.

Turn away from the breeze for shelter—and the playing of pipes.

A little preparation and reparation, and the earth nest is readied—the stubborn root knot patted with mud—the leaves piled readily.

The music is from our childhood and before. A nameless tune we learned before memory.

There might come dancers. And if they do we must let them be. If they do not we must watch the trees dance—and obey the still evening ourselves.

My nature has changed. My companions a few and I have little now to say to them.

That which they know they will recognize—that which they do not they will not. I need not offer the world to my fellow fauns.

The sound of water is our companion heart. It rains a little but our beards are greased.

Everything is an omen for everything will happen.

Dark house standing in a darker field

Mind is, after all, the almost unimaginably complex emergent quality of the languaged organism.

But you insist, I hear you, that when you close your eyes you can hold an image of something, of a face, somehow before you. How large is this image? Is it two inches across? Does it have an edge? How clear is it? Is it as distinct as you think, or are you relying on some kind of visual shorthand. And where is it located? It is a trick. You tell yourself you have seen it. This illusion seems fundamental to who you are in the universe, but it is a trick. How do the blind think? Do they resort to a mental smell? No, thought is language.

Language has conjured the bodies of a million ghosts. It is our dormant senses (particularly our ocular sense) that engage with such a performance to convince ourselves the dream has a body.

—W. Williamson, *Notes on Being.*

This schematism of our understanding, in its application to appearances and their mere form, is an art concealed in the depths of the human soul, whose real modes of activity nature is hardly likely ever to allow us to discover, and to have open to our gaze.

— Immanuel Kant, *Critique of Pure Reason.*

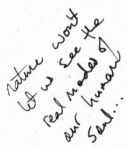

My Picture Left

I now think language deaf
Its sentence blind unconscious read
So much want these hundred hairs
My face his eyes her ears unsaid

—W. W.

our Death from Dark Oblivion
the great Day of our union
His providence shall <u>vindicate</u>
His pasture bright <u>immaculate</u>

—T. S.

I have regained some weight
About the bones—and light
Enters the house we have
Now mirrors frame the walls

An ant enters our cell
And whether conversation
Of his walk explains itself
Neither can tell

Corot drops brushes by the ground
To wade into the afternoon
Dark waters and the rushes
Of a mirror pond

—W. W.

<u>Five mirrors</u>

Having no more
Than this life
Of space and time
I despair
Of space and time
Than this life
Having no more

When you move
Towards me
With your smile
I hope for love
With your smile
Towards me
When you move

The slow current
Of brown and green
Some flashes of light
On the river surface
Some flashes of light
Of brown and green
The slow current

My young son
Forever away
When he left
With my heart
When he left
Forever away
My young son

This final morning
A brilliant sun
I see as if
Alive only just
I see as if
A brilliant sun
This final morning

He won't speak
On the phone
When I call him
To say I love you
When I call him
On the phone
He won't speak

Now apart
Though I love her
As ever
It is better
As ever
Though I love her
Now apart

When we fight
I love you
Made angry
By something small
Made angry
I love you
When we fight

I remember when all the animals in the zoo seemed to be in the moon. They were all roaring and howling together. There is a beautiful strong wind and we shall have no Zeppelins.

And when the self/pulled to the question of Identity/retreats—then we might know its honest aspect/ a shadow, coward of its own life—stranger to the direct gaze.
—William Swan, *Apocrypha of Being*

The maid took the trouble to lower herself backwards, which was a great courtesy.

The soul very well recognizes all elements being constituted minutely of the same.

The soul is made of the body as the impression is made of the wax.

Is it correct to assume that the soul of the river is made of water?

Goodness (god?) is manifest more in the workings of community than the individual deeds of a saint.

The moral grounding of your work will be most lasting. Your intentions are most obvious (moreso to others than yourself).

The Thirteen Book Habitation

A captive coming from a house
Half conscious dwelling underneath
What shall I take
The summer race of course
A place both slackening and resolute
Two in the afternoon
Behind my head
A tribute for unmanageable thoughts

travel

(Virgin Flight NYC–London June 16ᵗʰ, 2004)

Take this mark as evidence of Faith
In you and all your other selves
What we have held remains
Elsewhere—question the year
This moment started in a room
Banking the River—written in a place
Not any place—a blank page
At the end of The Prelude
Our portion is cheap
Intimate and clear
Another virgin flight

Dust as we are grows within the sphere
Work like a seethe, Impressed, stamped over
See Cowper, milk-white clusters, hazel-nuts
Rested on unsubstantial fabric torn
The Roman Empire topic of a paper bag
Picked out by invisible foundations of the wind

What then today you don't
Painting the river's volumes
Depth from surfaces retracts
The sunken amber globes (glow)
Destitute of purpose or of finishing this present task
Memory resolved—my thoughts composed
In Worcestershire, the birds this year (last year)
The blackbird here so far.

Mysterious damned Regal Woods
& weather—domiciles—the Terraced Rows
even the cobble stones
lay in untutored clarity

and we are swallow-souled for in its arcs and wheels we recognize that aspect of our highest self that soars in elevated mediums.
—Thomas Swan

and our soul is of foliage and standing ponds—the lofty elms—kissing the sand and the penny-loaf—the colour of amber crab-shells—and the pink-eared wheat flower. The fretful hare and docile kine...we are a street, a thousand people intermingled...we are dung, the airy firmament, a swarming thing we are—habitude to multiples, visitor of the far universe. Down to the depths of the ocean is our self-leviathan.
—Thomas Swan

Death of K.

Consumed in Rosa
Pink the dust of Rome
A lock of hair some bones
The climate critical
His death inspired
A library memorial
Burnt in a tiny urn
The original furniture
in February
On order of the Vatican

Song of the Swallow

It is this
Fever music
I exist

if it itself could empty of itself
like to a shell unshrowd
then on the ocean shelf it sat
and who would hear it say not dead aloud

But as you are but shell
robed in your shrewd activities
That when He says undone
out to himself it is a ringing bell

—T. S.

Gravitation, all in all / nothing in any one part, as fluid, ether, or such like / —analogy of this to *Soul,* to Consciousness / that nothing-something, something-nothing /
—Coleridge, *Notebooks*

M's Dream

Though never from ourselves
Retreat, nor hidden bide
We will irrational Ends
That which befell
Self—He who was given and received
The seed of Harvest all
Has now a dim shade cast
Our clamouring for honours
Flying in cacophonous mid air
Nor can we rest on spiteful heels
Our heated chairs our soft purchase(s)
Pillowed in indulgent (restless) sleep
But in our dreams our teethy towers
Crumble and our writ[h]ing bodies snake
In rhythm of our own abuse. Deny
Our bliss and hammer at a paltry
Toy—our efforts ruining work—
Our tiredness fatigue—our fear
Unchallenged and our end assured
In dismal option—freedom for
The choking envelopes of holy days
And Edens in aspect alone
The labourer's heel must spade
Through roots and ruinous foundations
For his fruit—silent to his own antithesis
Under no old name nor in secure
Bond—no college ties his wit
Nor patron offers order
He may grasp. But to his soil
And simple burial he works

His hours his own—his elements apparent
All efforts are exact—all sober
Air and light until his lapse
To ordinary earth and extraordinary breath

A dark disc is gulped down invisibly
Prior to our seeing—Instantly
the light reacts—by the water
's slow moving edge
We inspect layers of subaqua-luminosity
Instants of globe light lifted along the reed beds
Instants of cloud and leaf—instants
Of house and hogweed reflected instantly.
All this is to console the absent disc
Though in truth it prevents nothing—predicts nothing
My slowness of perception assumes loss. Never possess
Accuracy is asymptotal. I am writing on the earth.
And disappears. Presently.—

misread: My slowness of perception assumes nothing.

I am more convinced than ever
(as I write this) Of a self
moving towards
across something (a room, my room)
a page (imagine this stanza is still ——— *meta*
only 4 lines long)—which is incidentally
veldtland—a loamy meadow—face ←——— *good!*
against the carpetscape. I'm following
my own lead—supporting one ambitious self
encouraging the child to do its own thing
casually—on track—the great weight of history
Marguerita Isidore Seneschal
Tall Green Smooth Penis Woman
snagged inconsequentially on gorse.

language cracking now →

Close to the town square—arcaded
in a tourist hotel—or a back room
Is a struggle—shuffle upright in a
confined space—vigorous and quick. Repeat

their talk then is any
might happen on a subject
appropriate—casual, bright
without intimacy, upright

I've said it now
Reek of smoke—
Caustic blue
Restrained. tears. Release.

Where place is darkness?
or light abundantly?
can you uncover unions
through the gates uneven
Derby centre
Even a raven parent
She was softly rubbing things out
He was terrified of his violence
His face obliterated—teeth
Scintillating dawn—considering
The coordinates of his release

A solemn game

(Many boots and jacket made from yellow thunder
of hot corduroy—sweating in the damson enclosure
In a shallow dish a little tepid water is all I have to drink)

Diurnal

Succulent night—freaked
With fear and appetites
Un quenching—tuber stores
Grow palisades—cots
Grottoes palaces of stranger
States we almost know

Adored day—littered on the pool
Light generations—unrecognizable
Events as yet—what we might hope
Fortune numbers in the grass
Hair and the insect instantaneous

heavy

I manage to have written a number of books without
Starting perhaps
Here I start again

What are we to do with these people
Some we love, respect, know something of.

Those whose desire I have loved—or
I mean those whose love I desire

Of them I grow tired perhaps

Earlier. Perhaps not that much Earlier
I believed I might occupy a number of glamorous Houses.

If we have to choose, what criteria can we trust
As we change—are deflected—deflated—repeated.

The afternoon manages to be the most usual part of the day.

Domestic architecture—cheaply reproduced but functional.
Victorian artisan—a certain skill, a certain pride perhaps.

Those that are tired of their lives—those without a sense of
How to make a decision. They all have no time.

Those that are loved in success. How does it happen—
    for whom?
Where are my own simple pleasures? What did I give them
    away for?

Be vigilant—The same room in five years is not the same
room. You are shorter—your eyes dimmer.

For some reason—political acceptance—I have forsaken
The songs of beautiful girls.

Young men overcome their duty with energy.
Here I am again surveying the remnants of the slaughter.

One sees the hideous hermit crabs, four rayfish and
A red gunnet, wings tipped with violet and blue.

If you had time you might devise a method of escape
But you would never be brave enough to attempt it—even
Supposing that it might work.

The fate of Gilpin's Garden—
Shenstone shifted the river for his fountain—
The ground soaked up his inheritance
And he went to bed with bricks not books
To bury him goodnight.

M. imagines that
Stars might be
inhabited
Small plots
of fast-fading flowers
Called 'gardens of Adonis'
subject to mortality
hovering about the bridge
sleep in her animals
flies and the unknown
cloud descend—open
part of a lamp
poor thing
of what you speak
invisible.

The seat of the soul is the point where the inner and the outer worlds touch. Wherever they penetrate each other—it is there at every point of penetration

—*Novalis.*

In this allegorical dream
The old (older?) man
Began erasing words from his vocabulary
Eventually ending with (the word)

Perhaps the unconscious hangs out there, between people, as the speech that they produce between them, and are produced by...the unconscious as the unconscious of language cannot be internal, deep and half-hidden, like some modern version of the soul. If it is linguistic, then it is external.

—Denise Riley, *Words of Selves*.

A phantasmagoric image of the mind
An impression of endless thoroughfares
And innumerable peoples all apparently
In a desperate hurry to do something—
A labyrinth of streets and wilderness of walls
Swarming with beings, out of bounds
A lunacy of traffic—all history known and unknown
That mighty, monstrous London
Ever presently (to the mind) all avenues
High and Castle and Endless Street
White Hart, Angel, Packhorse, Greenman
St. Jude's, St. Swithin's, St. Bart's, St. Anne's
Blue-eyed, light-haired—thin armed.

<u>Simultaneously he writes of the ghost he follows:</u>

Opening on time again—in order to mark
Catching the merest
Converted warehouse—bookshop
The young man offers for sale
Ill-fitting jacket—white fleshed
Milk monitor—the Industrial Revolution
Along with areas of agricultural serfdom
Present in our own times.

The Pause indicates a deliberate break
An instant of sufficiency (comparable to closure)
Or of damage limitations
His idea is to return at another time
To rearticulate exactly that particular visitation
Differently exposed (conflict: vision interrupted)

I had a studio (you have to have this
Routinely, to visit over the course of months, years)
Though I was moved intermittently
Where I furnished the walls to resemble a studio
And here it was my practise to make paintings
(assuming, I suspect, that at some later date
I might take up the medium in true fashion).

Before this I had not recognized when my art happened.

Cryptogogic Glossolalia

Prophecy of the denounced Pentateuch
(speculating sensations)
Instant Interregnum, God Falls.
in the space between I and the say-word
I stands for proximity (temporal/spatial)
I manners of clouding—opportunity to
I progress—Memory of—Sleep
I beach approach—cobbled—articulates
I body members parts—focused on
I object(s) of desire—pen knife
I girlfriend, success (as seen)
Collared for the photograph—Which
defining moment—they don't recall
displaced now into the future of the photo-event
Jesus was an acolyte—Or The Paparazzi
Unpopular as guilt—What is German for Bumblebee
German Bumblebee (look it up)—A sculptor (Physician)
Dedicated to the single project of depicting human expression
Physiognomic distortion such as the sneeze withheld—
Or the unpleasant odour. What is the isolated voice
I wonder.

beach of memory

YES

The monsters have come loose
Broken glass (face somehow)
Allows—discord they
Prefer the others (a broken jar say)

A ship pitches (on the waves etc.)
Very much like a model
Decisions about boats
Leaning to one side

I'm writing about fucking villages again
(cheap red wine)

That man again
No head
For pornography
Avoids his fascinations
(with the Spanish tongue)

the whole book resembles
a poem—from
beginning to end

At the furthest reaches of self, that border where otherness begins, just at that place where the particles from one organizing entity mingle with those of another, what is it that reminds the soul of its body?

" this reminds me of "

vs.

" REMEMBER "

Gently those must listen
To the songs they mutter softly
Nor have they else their dwelling
As constantly as spring

Brothers live like cares
In palaces or caves
And death pursue their trades
More sweetly than all others

Praise even the torment
Old suffer in their hearts
The home of driven fear
Who listens to our song

Where the flesh of one body is indiscernible from that of another.

Murmuring tomb by grass and by the water
Appointed as enclosed on all sides by the night
Produced in May a young lamb driven here
Bless the abode—our speaker mixed with milk
We stretched here by the bank we drink and eat in summer/
dress in silk

quo pinus ingens albaque populus
umbram hospitalem consociare amant
ramis? quid obliquo laborat
lympha fugax trepidare rivo?

Q. HORATI FLACCI CARMINVM LIBER SECVNDVS

Why do the tall pines and pale poplars
love to embrace their branches in
inviting shade? Why does the rushing
water tremble through its winding banks?

Although the human spirit puts on airs
Boasting of Plato's doctrine that it is
An emanation of the heavens, yet
Without a body it remains inert

Seeing through the senses, hearing bodies
And imagining through offices
Our occupying spirit invents all
those matters that the body animates

You love the spirit and without a thought
Say the body pollutes love
But that's just spirit's little game

Embracing what is false instead of known
Like Ixion—who satisfied by air
Fell in love with nothing but a cloud.

(*from* Ronsard, Sonnet L from *Le Premier Livre des Sonnets
pour Hélène*)

Bell open flourishing
    Verdant song
Along the river bank
You are dressed
Just so
In wild vines

Two camps of red ants
Garrison your roots
Down your cracked trunk
All along
The bees make their nest

insects

The singing nightingale
Young
Courts his true-love
Pours his love-pang
Each year
In your leafy boughs

(*from* Ronsard, Les Odes)

Come just as we see the rose in May
In beauty young, the first flower
Render the sky a jealous grey
When Dawn cries on her

Grace in the petals, a well of love
Kiss the garden and the trees with scent
But beaten with a rain or heat
Petal by petal spent

As in your first flush
When the earth and heaven honour you
The Fates have made you dust

Receive my tears, this bowl
Of milk, these flowers
So that alive and dead your body is a rose

(*from* Ronsard, On the Death of Marie)

Where the extremities of thought engage with that furthest region of self-becoming-other, the soul's remotest limb.

This is the world I lived in
After I have died
A jettisoned soul
Despair flattened—

I cannot tell you how
It happened
One day everything
Is turned over—
This is how it looks
when I am dead

Soul Flesh
Off the main thoroughfare
On Merton Street
On a long table
Depending on the day
a cake
its form is everywhere in the house
and nowhere in particular
Herophilus declared these empty spaces
House the intellect—
Liver blood rushes to the marvelous network
Roofed with vaults of flesh
The vegetative soul of the liver
The vital soul of the heart
The rational soul of the head
Moving through the cosmos
Without supervision or purpose
Epicurus carried on
Leaked from the body
Death is therefore
Nothing to us
Anatomists marveled
A ball rolling on a perfectly flat table
The world had to become a machine
Monsieur N. Monsieur N would give him a melon
From another country. The melon must represent
His solitude since leaving France
Particles replacing souls

I was not a remarkable fellow. I don't even know what it is that
remarkable fellows are discovering just now. All I can do is try to
make this art as it appears to want.

which directed the flow
through the ventricles
for days in bed
vomiting phlegm
raving to god about the misery of man
"Now the hour has come
when you must leave your prison"
These thoughts could just as easily have been a sign
That the boy walking through the meadow
was destined for a quiet life
Each organ was linked to a heavenly body
The sun to the heart
And as soon as it entered a house, it ran through the same
The meadows through which he had walked to school as a boy
Became a war zone
   The school of Law was filled with supplies of corn
   The school of Astrology with soldier's uniforms
   The school of Rhetoric with rope bridges
The motion of the heart dedicated to the college
Death disturbed the body
Blood whirling pointlessly in a circle
The faculties of the fallen died with them
The soul itself bubbled up.

The thirteen Book Habitation (Regenerated)

First Part—the fairest of all rivers—
Song his song went shallow traveling
Dim in the shade but dwelling
When composed—breathing the fields and groves

The language of poetry is infinitely open, and as such is a model of the divine soul.

It dawned on me that I know nothing
all matter began as water
the willow was transmuted water
ferments were responsible for all changes in nature
Reason was a disease of the soul
He had nowhere else to go
So he became invisible
Introducing his countrymen to their new solar system
A Zoo, a botanical garden, a vast library, a laboratory
For what is the heart but a spring
The first organ of sense is touched and pressed
The library which had only half a dozen books
He passed the burned husks of houses
The crumbling earthen walls
He traveled out into the countryside

Then soul waits in the deep water for the light to penetrate
　　　—waits in the shallow shade for the light to turn
　　　—in the evening attains great height over the town
　　　—and is lost to our recollections of night
(If I could imagine a universe like this, the details)
　　　—hanging scent—offspring

(Not quite getting the head on right
　　　My real life is waiting between moments there of you)

(Somehow people could lose control of their bodies
　　　I don't believe you believe
　　　And I myself as yet far from land)

The Thirteen Book Habitation

That which is away from I partake of
In sympathy the bee and flower—and
Ill without my landscape—thyme and sage
Required—fish from these streams—those
Conscious of myself and of some other
Sound—a crow across a corn field...field

I returned to my homeland, not quite sure of my safety
Doing away with everything beyond the world of matter
And an abiding faith in the spirit world
The brain a hazy globe of notions on their way to other organs
It was fine to map the moon with ink invisible
Suddenly he felt utterly unprepared for the moment
When the morning came with clear quiet skies
And a perpetual suspicion he had not yet found truth
Fire, air, water, earth combine in a cup of tea
Tracing in those forsaken mansions
the inimitable work of the omniscient architect

The soul waits for a pang of Nostalgia
     —remembers a colour particularly
     —brushes past its incoming self

The soul's energy is not original
     —is of the body
     —which is not original

The mask—is exquisite
     —is ill-fitting
     —which is revealing

If you are between two (for example) instants
     —the occasion of recognition
     —uncertain

Exhaustion rising from the earth
     The common acceptance of Human Beings laid aside
     A waft of death came against him

Transcribing the momentous sentence (no nearer than the voices are).

(As much or as little as these fragments suggest, they do, it might be allowed, manage a brief history of the soul.

These small admissions do not matter at all. The great thing is to continue, mooning about the garden, teacup in hand, life hand in hand with death, for it is death I have been writing about all this time, that of which we are always thinking, that which is the only resolution to our thoughts.)

book

—W. W., *This Fatal Looking Glass*

We live at the bottom of an Ocean of the element air
—Torricelli

To keep the heart beating—to remember the world—to learn
the ability to conceive of oneself or of God or of anything not
immediately before the senses.

The clothes of the self are garments of the world. When we
articulate selfhood it is an instant of general existence, when we
whisper secrets of selfhood in the hidden rooms of the mind it
is a metaphor from the world—utilizing that which all mortals
borrow—reconstituting the molecules of existence.
—William Swan, *Apocrypha of Being*

In Volume XIII of his *Moralia* Plutarch holds that according to Plato, God literally brought into being the soul and the body of the Universe, though not from nothing, which is impossible, but from precosmic principles that had always existed, an amorphous and chaotic corporeality and a self-moved and irrational motivity that kept the former in disorderly turmoil.

According to the *Mundaka Upanishad,* Spirit is the Creator of the god of creation.

Anselm believed if God existed in the mind he must exist in the real world

Liebniz contrasted the actual world with an infinity of merely possible worlds

First, the Baroque differentiates its folds in two ways, by moving along two infinities, as if infinity were composed of two stages or floors: the pleats of matter, and the folds in the soul...Clearly the two levels are connected (this being why continuity rises up into the soul)...When we learn that souls cannot be furnished with windows opening onto the outside, we must first, at the very least, include souls upstairs, reasonable ones, who have ascended to the other level ("elevation"). It is the upper floor that has no windows. It is the dark room or chamber decorated only with a stretched canvas "diversified by folds."...Folds are the soul and authentically exist only in the soul...they are virtualities, pure powers whose act consists in habitus or arrangements (folds) in the soul...the whole world is only a virtuality that currently exists only in the folds of the soul which convey it...the soul is the expression of the world (actuality), but because the world is what the soul expresses (virtuality).
—Gilles Deleuze, *The Fold: Leibniz and the Baroque.*

So it is that matter and soul inhabit the same house. We cannot see into the enfolded soul. Its cause is our own. We can only read it as we might a poem, that folds upon itself infinitely. We dream of a realm beyond our sensory grasp, a culmination of our senses perhaps, a place we notice only through the ride around the surface. Reading is a combination of seeing and moving, of remembering and thus imagining.

...thick layerings, offering the tiny tomb, surely, of the soul
—Stéphane Mallarmé, *Le Livre, Instrument Spirituel.*

Imagine the soul is a fabulous many-formed monster of antiquity. This beast has the heads of tame and wild animals that it can grow out of itself and transform at will. A lion and a man. Contained in our outward body. A conflict ensues.

A two horse chariot—one noble one unruly. The dark horse is appetite.

Where does the soul abide?

As one who hangs down-bending from the side
Of a slow-moving boat upon the breast
Of a still water, solacing himself
With such discoveries as his eye can make
Beneath him in the bottom of the deeps,
Sees many beauteous sights (weeds, fishes, flowers
Grots, pebbles, roots of trees) and fancies more,
Yet often is perplexed and cannot part
The shadow from the substance—rocks and sky,
Mountains and clouds, from that which there abide
In their true dwelling—now is crossed by gleam
Of his own image, by a sunbeam now,
And motion that are sent he knows not whence,
Impediments that make his task more sweet;
Such pleasant office have we long pursued
Incumbent o'er the surface of past time
With like success. Nor have we often looked
On more alluring shows (to me at least),
More soft, or less ambiguously descried,
Than those which now we have been passing by,
And where we still are lingering.
—William Wordsworth, *The Prelude*, 1805

But the sound of water escaping from mill-dams, etc., willows, old rotten
planks, slimy posts, brickwork, I love such things…As long as I do paint, I
shall never cease to paint such places.
—John Constable, *Letter to John Fisher,*
   Hampstead, October 23rd, 1821

(The last picture he painted, and on which he was engaged on the
last day of his life, was a mill, with such accompaniments as are
described in this letter.)

The whole of Nature is a metaphor of the human mind
—Emerson

Walking along the road he turned his head and looked into
heaven—with, at home, a portrait of Father (disappeared) and a
portrait of himself (disappeared)—in the air diagonally <u>toing</u> and
<u>froing</u> between the cypress trees.

The soul that issued forth seemed to me quite naked...in the appearance of a child...the creature was a tiny figure...as green as a chive...its expression distinct, but anymore I could not say...only that it left in a resigned fashion, with the affect of obedience.

The pre-Socratics placed thought inside Caverns and life
   in the deep.
Platonism looked to ascend.
But the Cynics and Stoics operated instead "where there is no
longer depth or height."

Let us return to the surface of a pond.
Elements touch—
Vastnesses reflected and supported—
Vastnesses implied and contained—
Nothing is hidden.
All expands infinitely—atomistic and ever-forming in unity.

Language lives on the surface—unconsciousness withdraws
from and overtakes the spoken (which evolves into the written).
Consciousness is light on the surface, reflected or projected.

The surface is immediate and impenetrable—penetration merely extends
   the surface.
The surface trembles with possibilities—with elemental life.
Everything is played out on this dimension.

The surface is constantly moving into and out of being. Being
is not apprehensible, just as the surface avoids apprehension.
Apprehension is another aspect of the surface—of being.

And in the midst of this wide quietness
A rosy sanctuary will I dress
With the wreath'd trellis of a working brain...
—Keats, *Ode to Psyche*

Wittgenstein denied the philosophical tradition that consciousness was somehow 'inner.' For him consciousness played upon the 'outer' surface without any mystery.

Zettel 220: *Consciousness in another face. Look into someone else's face, and see the consciousness in it, and a particular shade of consciousness. You see on it, in it...*

"Dasein is not a spatial interiority, the secondary nature of which would have to be derived from a becoming-spatial. It has its own being-in-space... One must not say that being-in-a-world is a spiritual property. One must not say that man's spatiality characterizes his body alone."
—Jacques Derrida

And Likewise:

"Spirit does not fall into time, but it exists as originary temporalization."—Martin Heidegger

Thus spirit is not separate from being in space and being in time, but is rather that which allows dimension and duration.

Consciousness, feelings, emotion, mind, ego, spirit, soul, pain etc. These words are habits of thousands of years of mistaken belief…We have to believe that consciousness does not exist; indeed, there is no reason to believe that it ever did exist.
—By the Late John Brockman

The Mind or Soul, we are often told, has three parts, namely, Thought, Feeling and Will; or, more solemnly, the Mind or Soul functions in three irreducibly different modes, the Cognitive mode, the Emotional mode, and the Conative mode. This traditional dogma is not only not self-evident, it is such a welter of confusions and false inferences that it is best to give up any attempt to refashion it. It should be treated as one of the curios of theory.
—Gilbert Ryle, *The Concept of Mind.*

rare, unused, intriguing object.

We must give up the notion of this organism as made of a bit of res cogitans nonspatially associated with a bit of res extensa.
—Richard Rorty, *Philosophy and the Mirror of Nature.*

extended thing

We should do well to commiserate our mutual ignorance
—John Locke

Carver...could almost have imagined that his boat was suspended in an element as pure as air, or rather that the air and water were one....

The water of the English lakes...being of a crystalline clearness, the reflections of the surrounding hills are frequently so lively, that it is scarcely possible to distinguish the point where the real object terminates, and its unsubstantial duplicate begins...

not to speak of the fine dazzling trembling network, breeze motions and streaks and circles of intermingled smooth and rippled water, which make the surface of our lakes a field of endless variety.
—William Wordsworth, *Description of the Scenery of The Lakes*

Matter is infinitely porous, with a system of caverns endlessly contained therein: even the densest element offers a reservoir in potency—avenues and rivers, harbors and hidden pools. Here light colours the many contours uniquely...consider the human body, filled as it is with cavities and capacities...the soul inhabits matter as a fish in a stream, a breath in its lung, a mole in the soil.
—Thos. Swan

The surface isn't so much dimensionless as it is the field of multi-dimensional interaction.

Depth is the apperception of the multiplicity of surface—We imagine depth as the store of surface interaction. If surface relates to the present then depth is its temporal distortion into past and future.

Surface does not disclose itself.
—William Williamson

If God is, it is because He is in the book. If sages, saints and prophets exist, if scholars and poets, men and insects exist, it is because their names are found in the book.
—Edmond Jabés, *Book of Questions*

When the writer is about to drown in the ocean of the blank page, it is the word allows him to swim, to stay on the surface.
—Rosmarie Waldrop

When we go but one step beyond the immediate sensible qualities of things, we go out of our depth.
—Edmund Burke, *A Philosophical Enquiry etc.*

Once more following the Evening's blue lament
along the hill, along the springtime pond—
as if the long dead Shadows hover over,
shades of stately clerics, noble dames,
their flowers bloom grave violets in soil—
whisper crystalline blue waves,
sacred groves of oaks grow green
over forgotten pathways of the Dead
the golden cloud reflected on the pond.

(*from* Georg Trakl *Wieder folgend der blauen Klage des Abends*)

Shelley's journeys after what he never found have racked his purse and his tranquility

Young men might need to sail and sink

(*Narcisse upon the wat'ry bank...*)

The Art of Flying

In common with the wider race the idea of flying the most
promising way of seeing the heavens—to sustain one's self like a
bird. Out of the window—like a leaf on the still air—a portrayal
of the night sky. Paschendaele and Gheluveldt: a slow pantomime
nightmare—traversing Romney Marsh—I began, for instance, to
explore depth—colour relationships—and realized these were my
first attempts to fly.

Is there a possibility that I'm a monad—an individual thing having no proper parts?
—Roderick M. Chisholm

There is something adrift in thinking that consciousness can exist as something in its own right.
—Susan Greenfield

separate

When we turn the senses towards our own body, and become conscious of our bodies as we might of some other outward object, such as a book, and we naturally understand the body to be of the same order as that other object, something quite distinct from the self perceiving—and so it is we construct a metaphorical habitation for the self apart from the body, this habitation we construct to house the self during such perceptions is called soul. <u>Soul is a narrative of self-conscious consciousness,</u> a tool of the functioning body, most specifically the brain.
—William Williamson, *Notes on Being*

The construction of poems becomes the record of a series of individual thresholds of the experience of being conscious; they form the definitions, or affirmation, in time and in language, of human identity.
—Veronica Forrest-Thomson, *Note*

The poem occupies consciousness, or consciousness occupies the poem. The poem might be seen as a temporary body, an armature, just as anything in the world demanding attention might. What seems special about the poem is the significance of its self-conscious (or if you prefer self-reflexive) construction. In this aspect it resembles a human. The vehicle was made to be driven. The instrument was made to be played upon.

Man is an instrument over which a series of external and internal impressions are driven, like the alternations of an ever-changing wind over an Æolian lyre, which move it by their motion to ever-changing melody…it is as if the lyre could accommodate its chords to the motions of that which strikes them, in a determined proportion of sound; even as the musician can accommodate his voice to the sound of the lyre…and…the lyre trembles and sounds after the wind has died away…to prolong also a consciousness of the cause.

—Shelley, *A Defence of Poetry*.

Dear Jane/The guitar was tinkling/But the notes were not sweet till you sung them/Again…So your voice most tender/To the strings without soul had then given/Its own.

—Shelley, *To Jane*

My lute be still, for I have done
—Sir Th^os. Wyatt

Blame not my lute, for he must sound
—Sir Th^os. Wyatt

*As a fool seeks for the abode of music in the body of the lute, so does he
looks for a soul within the body and mind of the individual*
—Siddhartha Gautama

The past seemed almost inevitable

The horizon is where the eyes run out

Not the author but a copy of his own book

It is, as it were, the presence of the absent,
such as we feel
in contemplating a familiar empty chair.

time

death

identity

Space

not ourselves, but that

Fence Books

MOTHERWELL PRIZE

living must bury	Josie Sigler
Aim Straight at the Fountain and Press Vaporize	Elizabeth Marie Young
Unspoiled Air	Kaisa Ullsvik Miller

ALBERTA PRIZE

The Cow	Ariana Reines
Practice, Restraint	Laura Sims
A Magic Book	Sasha Steensen
Sky Girl	Rosemary Griggs
The Real Moon of Poetry and Other Poems	Tina Brown Celona
Zirconia	Chelsey Minnis

FENCE MODERN POETS SERIES

Nick Demske	Nick Demske
Duties of an English Foreign Secretary	Macgregor Card
Star in the Eye	James Shea
Structure of the Embryonic Rat Brain	Christopher Janke
The Stupefying Flashbulbs	Daniel Brenner
Povel	Geraldine Kim
The Opening Question	Prageeta Sharma
Apprehend	Elizabeth Robinson
The Red Bird	Joyelle McSweeney

NATIONAL POETRY SERIES

The Network	Jena Osman
The Black Automaton	Douglas Kearney
Collapsible Poetics Theater	Rodrigo Toscano

ANTHOLOGIES & CRITICAL WORKS

Not for Mothers Only: Contemporary Poets on Child-Getting & Child-Rearing
Catherine Wagner & Rebecca Wolff, editors

A Best of Fence: *The First Nine Years,* Volumes 1 & 2
Rebecca Wolff and *Fence* Editors, editors

POETRY

English Fragments / A Brief History of the Soul	Martin Corless-Smith
The Sore Throat & Other Poems	Aaron Kunin
Dead Ahead	Ben Doller
My New Job	Catherine Wagner
Stranger	Laura Sims
The Method	Sasha Steensen
The Orphan & Its Relations	Elizabeth Robinson
Site Acquisition	Brian Young
Rogue Hemlocks	Carl Martin
19 Names for Our Band	Jibade-Khalil Huffman
Infamous Landscapes	Prageeta Sharma
Bad Bad	Chelsey Minnis
Snip Snip!	Tina Brown Celona
Yes, Master	Michael Earl Craig
Swallows	Martin Corless-Smith
Folding Ruler Star	Aaron Kunin
The Commandrine & Other Poems	Joyelle McSweeney
Macular Hole	Catherine Wagner
Nota	Martin Corless-Smith
Father of Noise	Anthony McCann
Can You Relax in My House	Michael Earl Craig
Miss America	Catherine Wagner

FICTION

Flet: A Novel	Joyelle McSweeney
The Mandarin	Aaron Kunin

*egotism   *"poet   *S.R.

(Performers)

failed comedy routine
humor vs. poetry
↳ performing poem
vs.

Collab

breaking down
↓ progression

excessive? habitual?
push it further →

Vivis book = command of space
almost a kind of tension
that shes riding out ...

"talk among
yourselves &
gonna see if I can
find my slammers."

mechanism?
constraint?

Sincerity is a privilege.
programmatic
how can it be
sincere if it's
prescribed.

*Lisa
Robertson
"emergency"
quote

*Jasper Burns
chapbooks